Newcomer Book

Essential Vocabulary and Language Instruction for Newcomers

- Understanding School Language
- Understanding Instructions
- Making Requests

Scholastic Inc., 557 Broadway, New York, NY 10012.

Copyright © 2009 by Scholastic Inc.

All rights reserved.   Published by Scholastic Inc.   Printed in the U.S.A.

ISBN-13: 978-0-545-10394-7
ISBN-10: 0-545-10394-0

SCHOLASTIC, READ 180, LBOOK, SYSTEM 44, and associated logos and designs are trademarks and/or registered trademarks of Scholastic Inc.

Other company names, brand names, and product names are the property and/or trademarks of their respective owners.

4 5 6 7 8 9 10   08   16 15 14 13 12 11 10 09

Authors

Paula Leoni-Bacchus, Ph.D.

Paula Leoni-Bacchus holds a doctorate in bilingual/bicultural education
from Teachers College, Columbia University. For 15 years Dr. Leoni-Bacchus
taught ELD/ESL and Spanish as a World Language in U.S. public schools, and
in Mexico and Panama. She has also written professional development programs
and instructional materials intended to scaffold content-area subject matter for
English language learners.

Angel Alonso, M.S.Ed.

Angel Alonso taught high school ELD/ESL and fourth and fifth grade in
Holyoke and Boston public schools, and completed his degree in Elementary
Education at Wheelock College. Over the last ten years he has specialized in
developing materials and instructional programs for English language learners.

Advisor and Reviewer

Margarita Calderón, Ph.D.

Professor and Senior Research Scientist
Center for Research and Reform in Education
Johns Hopkins University

Use SAM resources to:

✔ Access the Newcomer Book answer key.

✔ Obtain tips, strategies, and RED research in the
Newcomer Book Teaching Guide.

 Resource Links
SAM Keyword: Newcomer Teaching Guide

Unit 3:
Your School and Community

Unit 4:
Your World

The Alphabet

The **alphabet** is all the **letters**. There are 26 letters in English. Learn the alphabet in English. Learn the name of each letter.

Aa Bb Cc Dd Ee Ff

Gg Hh Ii Jj Kk Ll Mm

Nn Oo Pp Qq Rr Ss

Tt Uu Vv Ww Xx Yy Zz

The Numbers

0	1	2	3	4	5
zero	one	two	three	four	five

6	7	8	9	10
six	seven	eight	nine	ten

ORAL PRACTICE

Read and Speak Take turns reading with a partner.

My name is Kim, K-I-M.   My phone number is 555-1468.

My name is Luis, L-U-I-S.   My phone number is 555-9372.

LANGUAGE DEVELOPMENT

How to Write Letters and Numbers

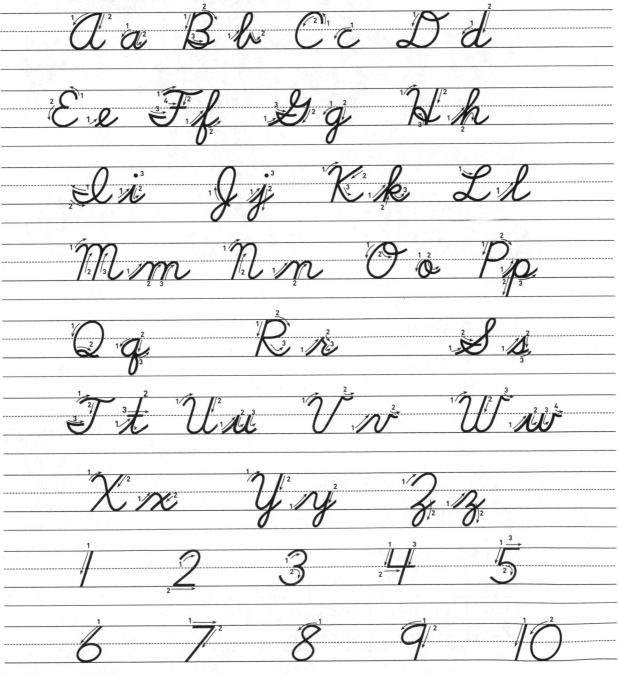

What's Your Name?

Hello.
My name is Lin.
What's your name?

Hi, Lin.
My name is Lucas.
It is nice to meet you.
How are you?

Photo credit: © Michael Newman/PhotoEdit.

CONCEPTS AND VOCABULARY

1. **Learn New Words** Say "Hello!"

Say **"Hello"** or "Hi" to a new **friend**.

Tell them your **name**.

Ask "What's your name?" or "What is your name?"

Say "It is nice to **meet** you."

Say **"Thank you."**

Other ways to say hello

Good morning!	before 12 noon
Good afternoon!	after 12 noon
Good evening!	after 6 P.M.

Vocabulary

friend
hello
meet
name
thank you

ORAL PRACTICE

2. Read and Speak Take turns reading with a partner.

Lin: Hello, my name is Lin. What's your name?

Lucas: My name is Lucas. It is nice to meet you, Lin.

Lin: It is nice to meet you, Lucas. How are you?

Lucas: I am fine, thank you. How are you?

Lin: Very well, thank you.

Lucas: It is nice to meet a new friend.

Complete the following sentences. Use vocabulary words.

1. Hello, my _____name_____ is Lin.
2. It is nice to _____ you.
3. _____, my name is Lucas.
4. It is nice to meet a new _____.
5. _____. It is nice to meet you, too.

LANGUAGE DEVELOPMENT

3. Read and Write Learn to use *am, are,* and *is.*

I	am
you	are
he, she, it	is

Complete these sentences. Use *am, are,* and *is.*

1. What _____is_____ your name?
2. My name _____ Lin.
3. How _____ you?
4. I _____ fine, thanks.
5. It _____ nice to meet you.

Now write four more sentences. Use *am, are,* and *is.*
Example: Hello, my name is Ming.

People and Places at School

CONCEPTS AND VOCABULARY

1. Learn New Words Read about people and places at school.

The **librarian** is in the library.

The **principal** is in the main office.

The **nurse** is in the health office.

The **coach** is in the gym.

The **students** are in the cafeteria.

The **teacher** is in the classroom.

Vocabulary

coach
librarian
nurse
principal
students
teacher

Places in school

hallway	where you walk from one room to another
cafeteria	where you eat lunch
auditorium	where special events take place

Photo credits: (clockwise) © Mark E. Gibson/Digital Railroad; © Tom Prettyman/PhotoEdit, Inc. © Michael Newman/

2. Read and Speak Take turns reading with a partner.

Luis: Hello, Susana. Where is the teacher?

Susana: Hi, Luis. The teacher is in the classroom.

Luis: And where is the principal?

Susana: The principal is in the main office.

Luis: Where is the nurse?

Susana: The nurse is in the health office.

Complete the following sentences. Use vocabulary words.

1. The _____teacher_____ is in the classroom.
2. The _____ is in the main office.
3. The _____ is in the library.
4. The _____ is in the health office.
5. The _____ is in the gym.

LANGUAGE DEVELOPMENT

3. Read and Write Learn to use nouns.

Nouns name people, places, and things.	teacher, librarian, nurse, principal, student, classroom, gym, office

Complete these sentences. Use nouns.

1. Where is the coach? The coach is in the _____gym_____.
2. Where is the principal? The principal is in the main _____.
3. Where is the librarian? The librarian is in the _____.
4. Where is the teacher? The teacher is in the _____.
5. Where are you? I am in the _____.

Now write four more sentences. Use nouns.
Example: The student is in the classroom.

READ180

The Classroom

screen

poster

mouse

headset

COMPUTER

book

desk

chair

monitor
or screen

keyboard

microphone

Photo credits: (left) © Roger Wyan; (right) © Dennie Cody.

CONCEPTS AND VOCABULARY

1. Learn New Words Read about your classroom.

There are many things in your classroom.

You sit at a **desk** during class.

You read a **textbook** to learn.

You also read on a **computer** to learn.

You write on **paper**.

Your teacher writes on the **board**.

Vocabulary

board
computer
desk
paper
textbook

More things in the classroom

bookshelf	chalk
chairs	posters
windows	map

2. Read and Speak Take turns reading with a partner.

Julio: Are you my teacher?

Ms. Jackson: Yes, I'm your teacher. My name is Ms. Jackson.

Julio: My name is Julio.

Ms. Jackson: It's nice to meet you, Julio.

Julio: It's nice to meet you, Ms. Jackson.

Ms. Jackson: This is your textbook, Julio. This is your desk.

Complete the following sentences. Use vocabulary words.

1. I sit at my _____ desk _____ during class.
2. I use a _____ to read stories.
3. I use _____ to write on.
4. I can use a _____ to read and write.
5. My teacher writes on the _____.

3. Read and Write Learn to use question words.

who	what
when	where
why	how

Complete these sentences. Use question words.

1. _____ When _____ does class start?
2. _____ is the cafeteria?
3. _____ is your teacher?
4. _____ is the restroom?
5. _____ is your favorite class?

Now write four more sentences. Use question words.
Example: Where is your classroom?

READ180

What We Do in Class

I read my book.

I write the answer.

I raise my hand.

Photo credits: (top) © Roger Wyan; (right) © Jeff Schultz/Alaska Stock

---

CONCEPTS AND VOCABULARY

 1. Learn New Words Read about the classroom.

In class, the teacher tells you what to do.

Read your book.

Wait for your turn.

Write the answer.

Take out your pencil.

Raise your hand.

Put away your book.

Line up at the door.

Vocabulary

line up
put away
raise
take out
wait

ORAL PRACTICE

2. Read and Speak Take turns reading with a partner.

This is what we do in school.

We read our books.

We raise our hands.

We take out our pencils.

We put away our books.

We line up at the door.

Complete the following sentences. Use vocabulary words.

1. If you have a question, please _____raise_____ your hand.

2. Please _____ your book.

3. Please _____ for your turn.

4. Please _____ at the door.

5. Please _____ your pencil.

LANGUAGE DEVELOPMENT

3. Read and Write Learn to use verbs.

Open your books.	**Raise** your hand.
Write the answer.	**Listen** to me.
Stop talking.	**Show** your work.

Complete these sentences. Use verbs.

1. Please _____show_____ me your homework.

2. Please _____ talking during class.

3. Always _____ your hand in class.

4. _____ your notebooks.

5. _____ to your teacher.

Now write four more sentences. Use verbs.

Example: Listen to your classmates.

What Time Is It?

8 A.M.
It's eight o'clock.

11 A.M.
It's eleven o'clock.

12 P.M.
It's noon.

10:15 P.M.
It's ten fifteen.

10:30 P.M.
It's ten thirty.

10:45 P.M.
It's ten forty-five.

CONCEPTS AND VOCABULARY

 1. Learn New Words Read about telling time.

We use a **clock** to tell **time**.

In the morning, we add the letters "A.M." to the time. We say "It's six A.M." In the afternoon and evening, we add the letters "P.M." to the time. We say "It's six P.M."

The middle of the day is twelve P.M., or **noon**.

The middle of the night is twelve A.M., or **midnight**.

| From 12:00 A.M. until 11:59 A.M., use "A.M." |
| From 12:00 P.M. until 11:59 P.M., use "P.M." |

Vocabulary

A.M.
clock
midnight
noon
P.M.
time

2. Read and Speak Take turns reading with a partner.

Julio: What time is it?

Ana: Look at the clock. It's eleven thirty.

Julio: It's 11:30 A.M. It's almost noon.

Ana: What time does class start?

Julio: Class starts at one fifteen.

Ana: After 1:15 P.M., we'll be in class.

Look at each clock. Write a sentence telling the time.

1. It is _____8_____ A.M.

2. It is _____ P.M., or _____.

3. It is _____ A.M.

4. It is _____ P.M.

5. It is _____ A.M.

1.

2.

3.

4.

5.

LANGUAGE DEVELOPMENT

3. Read and Write Learn to use *at*, *before*, and *after*.

at nine A.M.	**at** midnight
before eight thirty	**before** six P.M.
after two forty-five	**after** noon

Complete these sentences. Use *at*, *before*, and *after*.

1. I wake up _____at_____ six thirty A.M.

2. I usually go to sleep _____ ten P.M.

3. Class will start _____ eleven thirty.

4. I will call you _____ noon.

5. She was home _____ four P.M.

Now write four more sentences. Use *at*, *before*, and *after*.
Example: I am always hungry before noon.

Vocabulary

Fill in the circle next to the correct definition of the underlined word.

1. Please <u>raise</u> your hand if you have a question.
   - Ⓐ put up
   - Ⓑ put away
   - Ⓒ open
   - Ⓓ shake

2. We use the <u>alphabet</u> to write words.
   - Ⓐ numbers
   - Ⓑ paper
   - Ⓒ letters
   - Ⓓ board

3. I put my books in my <u>desk</u>.
   - Ⓐ computer
   - Ⓑ classroom
   - Ⓒ where you sit
   - Ⓓ office

4. Shake hands when you <u>meet</u> a new friend.
   - Ⓐ say "Thank you" to
   - Ⓑ say "Hello" to
   - Ⓒ very well
   - Ⓓ ask

5. The <u>librarian</u> works in the library.
   - Ⓐ nurse
   - Ⓑ person who takes care of books
   - Ⓒ teacher
   - Ⓓ person who works in an office

6. I go to sleep before <u>midnight</u>.
   - Ⓐ 12 P.M.
   - Ⓑ noon
   - Ⓒ 12 A.M.
   - Ⓓ clock

Read and Speak

Complete the blanks with *computer*, *time*, and *teacher*.
Then read the paragraph out loud.

My English _____ is very nice. Today she
helped us learn to tell _____ in English. After
that, she helped me use a _____ to do my work.
I really like my English class.

Language Development

Circle the word that best completes each sentence.

1. _____ were you late to class?

   Why   What

2. My teacher is in his _____.

   classroom   librarian

3. _____ your textbook to page 20.

   Open   Write

4. He _____ a new student.

   are   is

5. I will wait for you _____ school is over.

   at   after

Writing

On a separate sheet of paper, write five sentences about school.
Use *classroom*, *library*, *principal*, *textbook*, and *line up*.

What Do I Wear?

sweater

hat

vest

shirt

pants

shoes

sneakers

Photo credits: (left) © Rubberball/Getty Images; (right) ©Thomas Northcut/Getty Images.

CONCEPTS AND VOCABULARY

 1. Learn New Words Read about clothes.

The things you wear are called **clothes**. On a cold day, you might wear **pants**, a **shirt**, and a **sweater**. On a warm day, you won't need a sweater. You wear **shoes** or sneakers on your feet every day.

More clothes

hat	vest
coat	sneakers

Vocabulary

clothes
pants
shirt
shoes
sweater

ORAL PRACTICE

2. Read and Speak Take turns reading with a partner.

Lucas: It's a cold day.

Susana: I will wear warm pants.

Lucas: I will wear a warm shirt.

Susana: I will wear warm shoes.

Lucas: I will wear my sweater.

Susana: I will wear clothes that keep me warm.

Complete the following sentences. Use vocabulary words.

1. These new _____shoes_____ hurt my feet.

2. I wear a _____ when it is cold.

3. I wear a light _____ when it is warm.

4. I wear _____ or a skirt every day.

5. I like to wear nice _____.

LANGUAGE DEVELOPMENT

3. Read and Write Learn to use articles.

Indefinite Articles	Definite Article
a (used before consonants: **a** book, **a** hat)	**the**
an (used before vowels: **an** apple, **an** event)	

Complete these sentences. Use articles.

1. On a warm day, I don't wear _____a_____ coat.

2. I am wearing _____ shirt she gave me.

3. I like _____ clothes she wears.

4. I am wearing _____ old pair of pants.

5. I'm looking for _____ new pair of shoes.

Now write four more sentences. Use articles.
Example: I read the book he gave me.

What Are the Parts of Your Body?

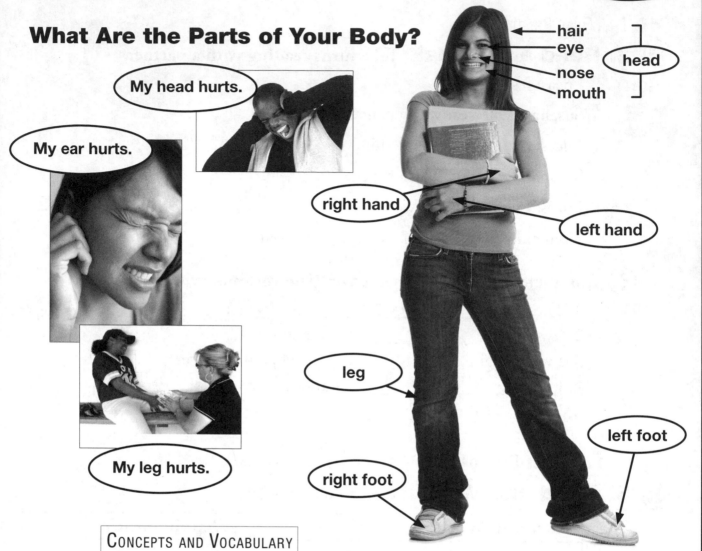

hair
eye
nose
mouth

head

My head hurts.

My ear hurts.

right hand

left hand

leg

left foot

My leg hurts.

right foot

CONCEPTS AND VOCABULARY

1. Learn New Words Read about the body.

What are the parts of your **body**? What do they do? You **see** with your eyes. You **hear** with your ears. You **smell** with your nose. You **taste** with your mouth. You **touch** with your hands. What else can your body do?

Parts of the body

head	eyes
mouth	nose
ears	hair
arms	hands
legs	feet

Vocabulary

body
hear
see
smell
taste
touch

Photo credits: (top left) © Cat London/iStockphoto; (center left) © Christina Kennedy/fStop/Getty

ORAL PRACTICE

2. Read and Speak Take turns reading with a partner.

I see with my eyes.

I smell with my nose.

I taste with my mouth.

I hear with my ears.

I touch with my hands.

I see, hear, smell, taste, and touch.

Complete the following sentences. Use vocabulary words.

1. I _____smell_____ with my nose.

2. I _____ with my eyes.

3. I _____ with my ears.

4. I _____ with my mouth.

5. I _____ with my hands.

LANGUAGE DEVELOPMENT

3. Read and Write Learn to use verbs.

Present/Past	Present/Past
use/used	smell/smelled
taste/tasted	hear/heard
see/saw	touch/touched

Complete these sentences. Use verbs.

1. I _____saw_____ that movie last year.

2. I _____ a good song last week.

3. I _____ with my ears.

4. I use my hands to _____.

5. I _____ my mouth to taste.

Now write four more sentences. Use verbs.
Example: I saw with my eyes.

What Is a Family?

father
Roberto

mother
María

grandmother
Alma

grandfather
Luis

Julio

uncle
Pedro

cousin
Marta

aunt
Ana

brother
Carlos

sister
Elena

Photo credit: © Rob Lewine/Corbis.

CONCEPTS AND VOCABULARY

1. Learn New Words Read about family.

A **family** is a group of people who live together. Who are the people in your family?

Julio has a **mother** and a **father**. He has a little **brother** and a big **sister**. Julio also has a grandmother and a grandfather, an aunt, an uncle, and a cousin.

Relatives

grandmother	mother's or father's mother
grandfather	mother's or father's father
uncle	mother's or father's brother
aunt	mother's or father's sister
cousins	uncle's and aunt's children

Vocabulary

brother
family
father
mother
sister

2. Read and Speak Take turns reading with a partner.

This is Julio's family.

María is Julio's mother.

Roberto is Julio's father.

Elena is Julio's big sister.

Carlos is Julio's little brother.

This is Julio's family.

Complete the following sentences. Use vocabulary words.

1. These are the people in Julio's _____family_____.
2. Elena is Julio's big _____.
3. Carlos is Julio's little _____.
4. María is Julio's _____.
5. Roberto is Julio's _____.

LANGUAGE DEVELOPMENT

3. Read and Write Learn to use adjectives.

> **Adjectives** tell **what kind** or **how many**.
>
> big, little, many, ten

Complete these sentences. Use adjectives.

1. There are _____ten_____ people in Julio's family.
2. Carlos is Julio's _____ brother.
3. Elena is Julio's _____ sister.
4. Julio is Elena's _____ brother.
5. Julio has _____ relatives.

Now write four more sentences. Use adjectives.
Example: This is my little cousin.

How Do You Feel?

surprised

tired

sad

afraid

smile

happy

CONCEPTS AND VOCABULARY

1. Learn New Words Read about feelings.

Your **emotions** are how you **feel**.

When you are **happy**, you **smile**. When you are **sad**, you do not want to smile. Happy and sad are emotions.

How do you feel today? Are you feeling happy or sad?

Emotions

happy	sad
scared	afraid
surprised	excited

Vocabulary

emotions
feel
happy
sad
smile

2. Read and Speak Take turns reading with a partner.

Today, I feel happy.

I want to smile.

Yesterday, I felt sad.

I did not want to smile.

I feel happier today.

It's good to have different emotions.

Complete the following sentences. Use vocabulary words.

1. Happy and sad are _____emotions_____.
2. Are you feeling _____ or _____?
3. How do you _____ today?
4. I feel happy. I want to _____.
5. I feel _____. I do not want to smile.

3. Read and Write Learn to use comparatives.

Comparative adjectives compare two or more things.
good, better, best
sad, sadder, saddest
happy, happier, happiest

Complete these sentences. Use comparatives.

1. I hope you feel _____better_____ than you did yesterday.
2. She felt _____ after losing the race.
3. I feel _____ today than yesterday.
4. Being happy is the _____ feeling I know.
5. It's _____ to understand your emotions.

Now write four more sentences. Use comparatives.
Example: I felt happier after I saw my friend.

Are You Hungry or Thirsty?

I'm thirsty.

fruit

milk

I'm hungry.

vegetables

sandwich

CONCEPTS AND VOCABULARY

 ## 1. Learn New Words

When you are **thirsty**, you need to **drink** something.

You can drink water, milk, or juice when you are thirsty. What do you like to drink?

When you're **hungry**, you need to **eat** some **food**.

You can eat fruit or a sandwich when you are hungry. What do you like to eat?

Foods	Drinks
salad	apple juice
hamburger	chocolate milk
vegetables	orange juice

Vocabulary

drink
eat
food
hungry
thirsty

ORAL PRACTICE

2. Read and Speak

Luis: Are you thirsty?

Susana: Yes. I am very thirsty. I need some water, please.

Luis: Yes, of course. Are you hungry, too?

Susana: I am a little hungry. Can I have an apple?

Luis: Yes. I will bring you an apple and water.

Susana: Thank you very much. That would be nice.

Complete the following sentences. Say them.

1. I am hungry. May I have some _____food_____ ?
2. What sort of food do you like to _____ ?
3. May I have a big sandwich? I am very _____ .
4. What do you like to _____ when you are thirsty?
5. May I have some water? I am very _____ .

LANGUAGE DEVELOPMENT

3. Read and Write Learn to use pronouns.

Singular Pronouns	Plural Pronouns
I eat, drink, need, like	**we** eat, drink, need, like
you eat, drink, need, like	**you** eat, drink, need, like
he, she, it eats, drinks, needs, likes	**they** eat, drink, need, like

Complete these sentences. Use pronouns.

1. My sister likes fruit. _____She_____ eats apples.
2. My brother likes milk. _____ drinks milk all the time.
3. My friends and I are hungry. _____ want to eat.
4. My cousins like apples and oranges. _____ like fruit.
5. You and I need to eat. _____ are hungry.

Now write four more sentences. Use pronouns.
Example: He likes to eat sandwiches.

Days and Months

Photo credit: © Image Source.

CONCEPTS AND VOCABULARY

1. Learn New Words Read about days and months.

A **week** has seven **days**: Sunday, Monday, Tuesday, Wednesday, Thursday, Friday, and Saturday.

A **month** has 28 to 31 days. A **year** has 12 months. There are 52 weeks in a year.

The months of the year are January, February, March, April, May, June, July, August, September, October, November, and December.

You can see days, weeks, and months on a **calendar**.

Vocabulary
calendar
days
months
weeks
year

seven days = one week
28 to 31 days = one month
twelve months = one year

2. Read and Speak Take turns reading with a partner.

Ms. Jackson: How many days are there in a week?

Luis: There are seven days in a week.

Ms. Jackson: How many weeks are there in a year?

Luis: There are 52 weeks in a year.

Ms. Jackson: How many months are there in a year?

Luis: There are twelve months in a year.

Complete the following sentences. Use vocabulary words.

1. I look at the ____calendar____ to see what day it is.

2. There are seven _____ in a week.

3. Every _____ has twelve months.

4. There are 52 _____ in a year.

5. The calendar shows all the _____ of the year.

LANGUAGE DEVELOPMENT

3. Read and Write Learn to use *in* and *on*.

on Monday	**in** December
on May 3rd	**in** the spring

Complete these sentences. Use *in* and *on*.

1. My birthday is _____in_____ January.

2. The party is _____ February 10th.

3. School starts again _____ Tuesday.

4. I will see you _____ the summer.

5. She will visit_____ June.

Now write four more sentences. Use *in* and *on*.
Example: We will see you on Thursday.

Vocabulary

Fill in the circle next to the correct definition of the underlined word.

1. I wear <u>shoes</u> to keep my feet warm and dry.
   - Ⓐ pants
   - Ⓑ things you wear on your feet
   - Ⓒ open
   - Ⓓ things you wear on your hands

2. Juice is good when you feel <u>thirsty</u>.
   - Ⓐ want to drink
   - Ⓑ food
   - Ⓒ hungry
   - Ⓓ happy

3. There are twelve months in a <u>year</u>.
   - Ⓐ seven days
   - Ⓑ 52 weeks
   - Ⓒ 31 days
   - Ⓓ calendar

4. There are four people in my <u>family</u>.
   - Ⓐ mother
   - Ⓑ mother's brother
   - Ⓒ father
   - Ⓓ a group of related people

5. When I feel happy, I want to <u>smile</u>.
   - Ⓐ look happy
   - Ⓑ feel
   - Ⓒ emotions
   - Ⓓ sad

6. I use my ears to <u>hear</u>.
   - Ⓐ touch
   - Ⓑ sense sound with your ears
   - Ⓒ emotions
   - Ⓓ feel

Read and Speak

Complete the blanks with *sad*, *brother*, and *shirt*.
Then read the paragraph out loud.

Soon my big _____ will go away to college.
This makes me feel _____, because I will miss
him. I will get him a present. I will hide it in the pocket of his
_____, so that he finds it later!

Practice Grammar

Circle the word that best completes each sentence.

1. _____ is my big brother.

      He   She

2. I need to buy _____ new coat.

      a   an

3. I like my English class _____ than my Math class.

      better   best

4. My friend has _____ relatives.

      many   how

5. Yesterday, I _____ something good cooking.

      smelled   smell

6. I will see you _____ two weeks.

      in   on

Writing

On a separate sheet of paper, write five sentences about things you
like to eat and drink. Use *thirsty*, *hungry*, *fruit*, *vegetables*, and *food*.

What's Your Favorite Class?

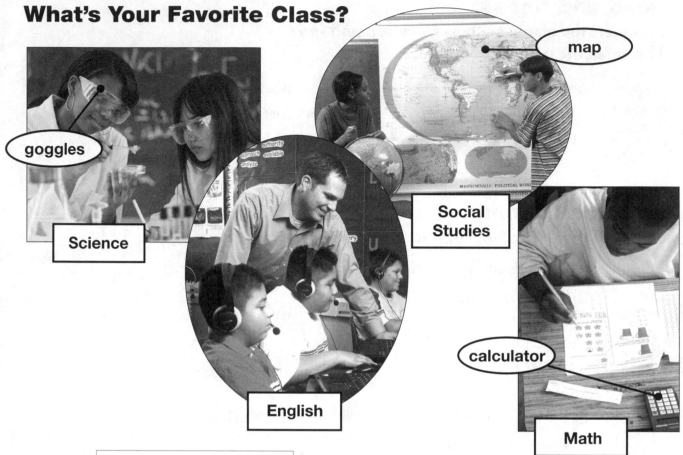

goggles

Science

map

Social Studies

English

calculator

Math

Photo credits: © LWA/Dann Tardif/Blend Images/Getty Images; © Roger

CONCEPTS AND VOCABULARY

1. Learn New Words

In math class, you learn to work with numbers. You also learn to **solve** problems.

In science class, you learn about the **Earth**, plants, and animals. You also **measure** things and do **experiments**.

In social studies class, you learn about the United States and the world. You also learn about **maps**.

In your English class, you learn to speak, read, and write in English.

Vocabulary

Earth
experiments
map
measure
solve

More classes

Drama
Music
P.E. (Physical Education)

ORAL PRACTICE

2. Read and Speak Take turns reading with a partner.

Susan: What's your favorite class?

Luis: Math is my favorite class. I'm good with math problems.
    Is math your favorite class, too?

Susan: No, it's not. My favorite class is science.

Luis: Why is that?

Susan: I'm good at doing experiments.

Complete the following sentences. Say them.

1. There is a _____map_____ of the U.S. in my social studies book.

2. Susan is good at doing _____ in her science class.

3. We used rulers to _____ our desks in math class.

4. You learn about the _____, plants, and animals in science class.

5. We use numbers to _____ problems in math class.

LANGUAGE DEVELOPMENT

3. Read and Write Learn to use contractions.

I am	I'm
you are	you're
he is, she is, it is	he's, she's, it's

Complete these sentences. Use contractions.

1. He is good with problems. _____He's_____ good with problems.

2. She is good at doing experiments. _____ good at doing experiments.

3. I am good with maps. _____ good with maps.

4. We are good in reading and writing. _____ good in reading and writing.

5. They are good with numbers. _____ good with numbers.

Now write four more sentences. Use contractions.

Example: I'm good in math.

Where Do You Live?

map

street

Photo credits: (left) © Nick Tzolov/iStockphoto; (right) © Robert Hollingworth/Alamy.

CONCEPTS AND VOCABULARY

 1. Learn New Words Read about giving directions.

Where do you **live**?
You need to know your **address**.
You need to know what **street** your school is on.
You need **directions** to help you get there.
A **map** can help you find a street.
A map can help you find an address.

Vocabulary

address
directions
live
map
street

Giving directions

Go straight.	Turn right.
Cross the street.	Turn left.

2. Read and Speak Take turns reading with a partner.

Susana: I'll meet you at the library. Where do you live?

Luis: I live at 325 East First Street.

Susana: What's the address for the library?

Luis: The library is at 97 West Second Street.

Susana: Can you draw a map or give me directions to get there?

Luis: Just walk three blocks down, then turn right. You'll find it.

Complete the following sentences. Use vocabulary words.

1. I don't know the _____address_____ for the library.
2. Can you give me _____ to get there?
3. Where do you _____?
4. I live on Park _____.
5. Here is a _____ to my house.

3. Read and Write Learn to use negatives.

don't	do not
isn't	is not
can't	cannot

Complete the following sentences. Use negatives.

1. No, that _____isn't_____ my address. (is not)
2. No, I _____ know where you live. (do not)
3. No, I _____ walk to your house. (cannot)
4. No, I _____ live near the school. (do not)
5. No, I _____ draw you a map. (cannot)

Now write four more sentences. Use negatives.
Example: I don't know your address.

City or Town?

suburb

city

town

Photo credits: (left) © Joseph Sohm/Corbis; (top right) © Walter

CONCEPTS AND VOCABULARY

 **1. Learn New Words** Read about places people live.

Where do you live? Do you live in a big **city**?
There are many **people** in a big city.
There are tall **buildings** in a big city.

Do you live in a small **town**?
There are not many people in a small town.
There are houses and buildings in a small town.

Do you live in a **suburb**, outside a big city?

city	busy, noisy, many people
town	quiet, fewer people
suburb	near a city

Vocabulary

buildings
city
people
suburb
town

ORAL PRACTICE

2. Read and Speak Take turns reading with a partner.

Do you live in a town, a city, or a suburb?

Many people live in big cities.

Many people live in towns, and others live in suburbs.

Is your city big and noisy? Does it have tall buildings?

Is your town small and quiet?

Do you like living in a city or suburb?

Do you like living in a town?

Complete the following sentences. Use vocabulary words.

1. My _____town_____ is small and quiet.
2. Are there tall _____ in your city?
3. Many _____ live in this city.
4. Is your _____ big and fun?
5. My aunt lives in a _____ outside of the city.

LANGUAGE DEVELOPMENT

3. Read and Write Learn to use correct word order.

| **Say:** My city is big. | **Ask:** Is your city big? |
| My town is small. | Is your town small? |

Complete the following sentences. Use correct word order.

1. My city _____is_____ big.
2. _____ your city big?
3. _____ town is small.
4. My suburb _____ nice.
5. My town _____ fun.

Now write four more sentences. Use correct word order.
Example: Is your city nice?

What Do You Need?

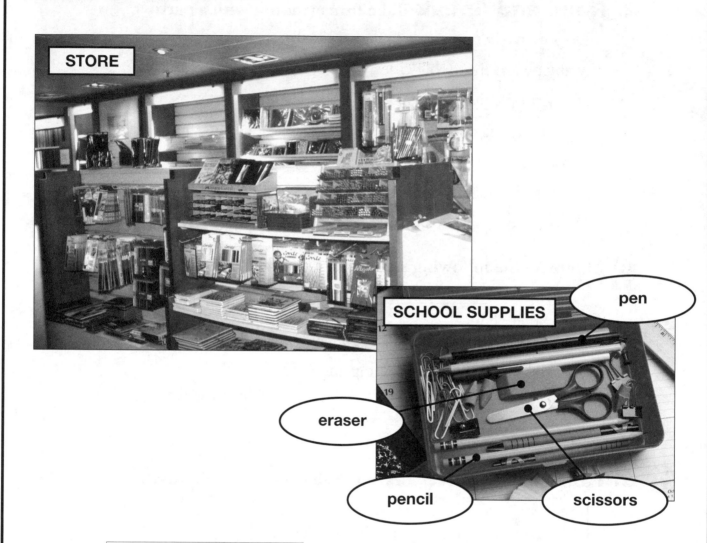

STORE

SCHOOL SUPPLIES

pen

eraser

pencil

scissors

Photo credits: (left) © Baumgartner Olivia/Corbis; (right) © Jeffrey Coolidge/Corbis.

CONCEPTS AND VOCABULARY

1. Learn New Words Read about shopping.

Where do you **buy** the things you **need** for school?
You can buy school supplies at a **store**.
You can buy notebooks and pencils at a store.
You go **shopping** for the things you need.
You **spend** money on the things you need.

More words about shopping

save	sale
expensive	cheap

Vocabulary

buy
need
shopping
spend
store

ORAL PRACTICE

2. Read and Speak Take turns reading with a partner.

Luis: I'm going to the store today.

Susana: I'm going shopping today, too.

Luis: What are you going to buy?

Susana: I need a new notebook.

Luis: My sister needs a new school bag.

Susana: Don't spend a lot of money!

Complete the following sentences. Use vocabulary words.

1. I will _____spend_____ money on a new notebook.

2. I _____ a new school bag.

3. We are going _____ today.

4. What will you _____ at the store?

5. What _____ is the best place to buy school supplies?

LANGUAGE DEVELOPMENT

3. Read and Write Learn about subject-verb agreement.

I	need
he, she	needs
I	spend
he, she	spends

Complete the following sentences. Use *need*, *needs*, *spend*, and *spends*.

1. She _____needs_____ a new notebook.

2. I _____ a new shirt.

3. She _____ a lot of money.

4. I _____ less money.

5. He _____ money to buy books.

Now write four more sentences. Use *need*, *needs*, *spend*, and *spends*.

Example: I need to buy food.

READ 180

How Much Is It?

$1
dollar bill

25¢
quarter

10¢
dime

5¢
nickel

1¢
penny

Photo credits: (left) © David Young-Wolff/PhotoEdit, Inc.; (top right)

CONCEPTS AND VOCABULARY

 1. Learn New Words Read about money and prices.

You use **money** to buy the things you need.
When you use money, you use **dollars** and **cents**.
You can buy clothes and food with money.
You can buy books and games.
When you buy something, you have to
know what the **cost**, or **price**, is.
That way, you know how much money you need.

Vocabulary

cents
cost
dollars
money
price

More words about money

coins	change
bills	credit

ORAL PRACTICE

2. Read and Speak Take turns reading with a partner.

Luis: What's the price of that bag?

Susana: It costs twelve dollars.

Luis: How much does that book cost?

Susana: It costs five dollars and fifty cents.

Luis: I don't think I will buy anything today. I want to save my money.

Complete the following sentences. Use vocabulary words.

1. How much does that bag _____cost_____?
2. What is the _____ of that notebook?
3. I have enough _____ to buy a bike.
4. The price is thirty _____.
5. I have one dollar and 25 _____, so I can buy a drink.

LANGUAGE DEVELOPMENT

3. Read and Write Learn about sentences and fragments.

Fragments	Sentences
ten dollars	It costs ten dollars.
buying that	I am buying that.
how much	How much does it cost?

Rewrite these fragments as complete sentences.

1. costs five dollars _____It costs five dollars._____
2. have enough money _____
3. the price is _____
4. that book _____
5. to save money _____

Now write four more sentences. Do not write fragments.
Example: *That book costs ten dollars.*

Workers in Your Community

police officer

waiter

x-ray

doctor

firefighter

mail carrier

construction worker

Photo credits: (clockwise): © Creatas Images/Jupiter Images; © Ben Fink/Foodpix/Jupiter Images; © Medioimages/Photodisc/

CONCEPTS AND VOCABULARY

1. Learn New Words Read about jobs and work.

A **job** is what someone does to **earn** money.
Workers in your community do many jobs.
A construction **worker** builds houses.
Workers in stores **sell** people the things they need.
A **police officer** helps direct traffic.

Vocabulary

earn
jobs
police officer
sell
worker

More jobs

mail carrier	firefighter
doctor	nurse
musician	waiter

ORAL PRACTICE

2. Read and Speak Take turns reading with a partner.

Luis: My cousin works in a restaurant. He's a waiter.

Susana: My brother is a doctor. He works in an office.

Luis: My father is a construction worker. He builds houses.

Susana: What sort of job would you like to do?

Luis: I would like to be a firefighter.

Susana: I would like to be a doctor.

Complete the following sentences. Use vocabulary words.

1. A _police officer_ helps direct traffic.
2. A construction _____ helps build houses.
3. Workers in stores _____ people the things they need.
4. A job is what someone does to _____ money.
5. Workers in your community do many _____.

LANGUAGE DEVELOPMENT

3. Read and Write Learn to use possessive pronouns.

my community	**her** house
your school	**our** restaurant
his job	**their** doctor

Complete the following sentences. Use possessive pronouns.

1. There are many workers in _____ community.
2. _____ favorite teacher is Ms. Chen.
3. _____ job sounds interesting.
4. _____ store is a good place to work.
5. _____ mother likes being a police officer.

Now write four more sentences. Use possessive pronouns.

Example: My uncle is a waiter.

Vocabulary

Fill in the circle next to the correct definition of the underlined word.

1. I live in a <u>city</u> with many parks and tall buildings.
- (A) map
- (B) large place with many people
- (C) give directions
- (D) find

2. I want to buy a new notebook at the <u>store</u>.
- (A) save money
- (B) place where you buy things
- (C) spend money
- (D) expensive

3. My uncle has a <u>job</u> selling cars.
- (A) in the city
- (B) worker
- (C) shopping
- (D) what you do to earn money

4. Luis likes to <u>solve</u> math problems.
- (A) measure
- (B) find the right answer
- (C) class
- (D) experiment

5. Can you give me <u>directions</u> to your house?
- (A) way to get to a place
- (B) drawing of an area
- (C) address
- (D) find

6. How much <u>money</u> will that cost?
- (A) buy something
- (B) what you use to pay for things
- (C) need
- (D) price

Read and Speak

Complete the blanks with *people*, *address*, and *town*.
Then read the paragraph out loud.

Where do you live? Do you live in a _____ or a city? Do many _____ live on your street? If you tell me your _____, I will come visit you.

Language Development

Circle the word that best completes each sentence.

1. They _____ live here any more.

    don't   isn't

2. How _____ does that shirt cost?

    many   much

3. _____ your town a fun place to live?

    Has   Is

4. She really likes _____ new job.

    her   she's

5. Susan likes science class. _____ good at it.

    You're   She's

6. We _____ to visit our grandparents.

    want   wants

Writing

On a separate sheet of paper, write five sentences about your city, town, or suburb. Use *street*, **buildings**, **people**, **shopping**, and **city**, **town**, or **suburb**.

What Season Is It?

CONCEPTS AND VOCABULARY

1. Learn New Words Read about seasons.

The **seasons** are **fall**, **winter**, **spring**, and **summer**.

Fall is in September, October, and November. Winter is in December, January, and February. Spring is in March, April, and May. Summer is in June, July, and August. We do different things in each season. In fall, we start a new school year. In summer, we can swim.

Vocabulary

fall
seasons
spring
summer
winter

Words about the seasons

fall	cool, fresh
winter	cold, snowy, windy
spring	warm, rainy
summer	hot, sunny, dry

Photo credits: © Ina Peters/Silberkorn/iStockphoto.

ORAL PRACTICE

2. Read and Speak Take turns reading with a partner.

In fall, the weather is cool. We can see the leaves change color.

In winter, the weather is cold. It snows in some places.

In spring, the weather is windy. We can fly a kite.

In summer, the weather is hot. We can go to the beach.

Fall, winter, spring, and summer.

These are the seasons of the year.

Complete the following sentences. Use vocabulary words.

1. In _____spring_____, the weather is windy.

2. In _____, the school year starts.

3. In _____, the weather is hot.

4. In _____, the weather is cold.

5. The year has four _____.

LANGUAGE DEVELOPMENT

3. Read and Write Learn to use indefinite pronouns.

anyone	anything
everyone	nobody
nothing	someone

Complete the following sentences. Use indefinite pronouns.

1. Can _____someone_____ please help me?

2. _____ wants to be inside today.

3. Do you know _____ about swimming?

4. There is _____ to do today.

5. Does _____ like winter?

Now write four more sentences. Use indefinite pronouns.
Example: Nobody likes the hot summer weather.

How Do You Get Around?

school bus

plane

car

train

bike

Photo credits: (clockwise) © Robin Nelson/PhotoEdit, Inc.; © Steve Allen/Brand X/Jupiter

CONCEPTS AND VOCABULARY

1. Learn New Words Read about transportation.

People travel from place to place. We use **transportation** to get around.

Some people ride a **bike** to school. Some people take the **bus**. Many people drive a **car** to get around. To go someplace far away, you may take a **plane**.

Vocabulary

bike
bus
car
plane
transportation

Other modes of transportation

taxi	subway
truck	train
car	motorcycle

2. Read and Speak Take turns reading with a partner.

Lin: How do you get around?

Lucas: I ride my bike.

Lin: How does she get around?

Lucas: She drives a car.

Lin: How do they get around?

Lucas: They take the bus. How do you get around?

Complete the following sentences. Use vocabulary words.

1. They take the _____ bus _____ to school.
2. There are many kinds of _____.
3. I ride my _____ to work.
4. She drives a _____ every day.
5. I take a _____ to visit my cousins.

LANGUAGE DEVELOPMENT

3. Read and Write Learn to use adverbs.

carefully	quietly
easily	slowly

Complete the following sentences. Use adverbs.

1. Please drive _____ carefully _____.
2. I can _____ give you a ride.
3. She opened the door _____.
4. They _____ ride their bikes to school.
5. He often talks too _____.

Now write four more sentences. Use adverbs.
Example: The bus goes slowly down the busy street.

What Region Do You Live In?

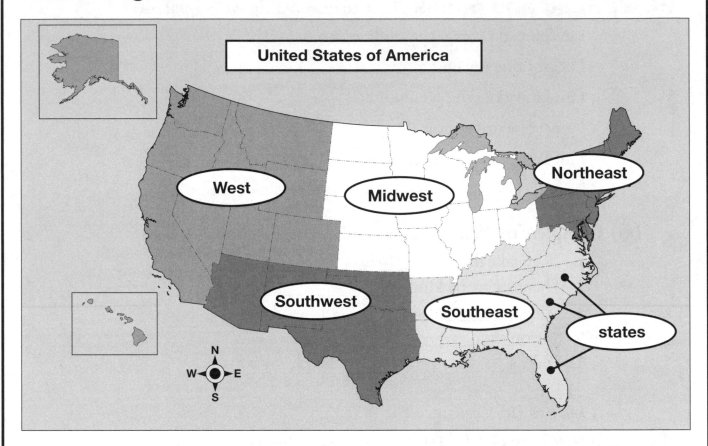

United States of America

West

Midwest

Northeast

Southwest

Southeast

states

CONCEPTS AND VOCABULARY

 1. Learn New Words Read about regions.

A **region** is a place or an area.
The map above shows five regions in the United States.
They are the **West**, the **Southwest**, the **Midwest**,
the **Southeast**, and the **Northeast**.
There are different states in each region.
What region do you live in?

Vocabulary

Midwest
Northeast
region
Southeast
Southwest
West

Facts about U.S. regions

There are fifty states in the United States.
48 of the states are connected to each other.
Two states (Alaska and Hawaii) are not connected to the others.

ORAL PRACTICE

2. Read and Speak Take turns reading with a partner.

Julio: There are five regions in the United States.

Lin: I live in the Midwest. I live in the state of Illinois.

Julio: My cousin lives in the Southeast. She lives in the state of Florida.

Lin: My friend lives in the Northeast. He lives in New York.

Julio: I have friends in the Midwest and the Southwest.

Lin: I have friends in many places, too!

Complete the following sentences. Use vocabulary words.

1. What _____region_____ do you live in?
2. I live in the _____.
3. The five regions are the West, the Midwest, the Southwest, the Southeast, and the _____.
4. Florida is in the _____.
5. California is in the _____.

LANGUAGE DEVELOPMENT

3. Read and Write Learn to use prepositional phrases.

at	**at** the airport
in	**in** this region
through	**through** the Midwest

Complete the following sentences. Use prepositional phrases.

1. I saw him _____at_____ the airport.
2. I like living _____ this region.
3. The plane flew _____ the air.
4. We met her _____ the bus stop.
5. You live _____ another state.

Now write four more sentences. Use prepositional phrases.
Example: I traveled through the South.

Important Americans

Susan B. Anthony

Rosa Parks

César Chávez

George Washington

Jane Addams

Martin Luther King, Jr.

Photo credits: (top left) © AP Images; (top center) © Bettmann/Corbis; (top right) © U.S. Postal Service Handout/AP

CONCEPTS AND VOCABULARY

1. Learn New Words Read about important Americans.

Many people have been an important part of American **history**. **Presidents**, men and women who work for equal **rights**, and writers and artists have all helped the United States.

We remember these **individuals** by creating **symbols**, such as paintings or statues of them. We name rivers, parks, and buildings after them. We celebrate their birthdays.

Vocabulary
history
individuals
presidents
rights
symbols

Some important Americans

George Washington was the first President of the U.S.
Susan B. Anthony helped women get the right to vote.
Jane Addams worked to educate immigrants and the poor.
Rosa Parks worked to end racial segregation.
Martin Luther King, Jr. worked for equal rights for all people.
César Chávez worked for civil rights for farmworkers.

2. Read and Speak Take turns reading with a partner.

Ms. Jackson: What important Americans do you know about?

Lin: I know about George Washington. He helped lead the country to independence.

Susana: I know about Susan B. Anthony. She helped women vote.

Luis: I know about César Chávez. He worked for the rights of farmworkers.

Julio: I know about Martin Luther King, Jr. He worked for equal rights.

Complete the following sentences. Use vocabulary words.

1. We celebrate the birthdays of American ___presidents___.
2. We remember _____ who helped the United States.
3. George Washington is an important part of American _____.
4. César Chávez worked for civil _____ for farmworkers.
5. Paintings and statues are _____.

LANGUAGE DEVELOPMENT

3. Read and Write Learn to use proper nouns.

People	Susan B. Anthony, Jane Addams
Places	United States of America, Washington, D.C.
Things	Declaration of Independence, Civil Rights Movement

Classify and categorize. Find four proper nouns and four common nouns on this page. Write them below.

Proper Nouns	Common Nouns
Ms. Jackson	presidents

Now write four sentences. Use proper nouns.
Example: George Washington was our first president.

How Does Our Government Work?

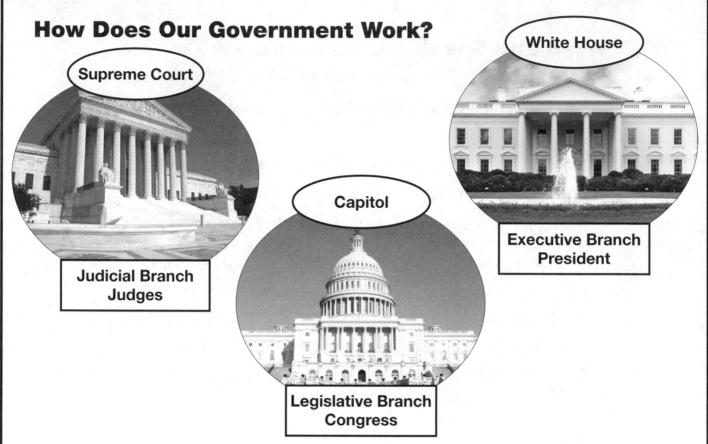

Supreme Court

**Judicial Branch
Judges**

Capitol

**Legislative Branch
Congress**

White House

**Executive Branch
President**

CONCEPTS AND VOCABULARY

 1. Learn New Words Read about American government.

The **government** of the United States has three parts, or branches: the **legislative**, **executive**, and **judicial**.

The legislative branch, or Congress, makes **laws**, or rules. The executive branch, or the president and his cabinet, makes sure the laws are followed. The judicial branch explains the laws.

All three branches follow the Constitution. The Constitution is the most important law in the United States.

Vocabulary

executive
government
judicial
laws
legislative

Three branches of government

legislative branch	Congress (senators and representatives)
executive branch	President (and his cabinet)
judicial branch	Supreme Court (judges)

2. Read and Speak Take turns reading with a partner.

Ms. Jackson: What are the three branches of government?

Lucas: They are the legislative, the executive, and the judicial branches.

Lin: The legislative branch makes the laws.

Susana: The executive branch makes sure that people follow the laws.

Luis: The judicial branch explains the laws.

Complete the following sentences. Use vocabulary words.

1. The President is the head of the _____*executive*_____ branch.
2. The legislative branch makes the _____.
3. The Supreme Court is in the _____ branch.
4. The _____ branch is also called Congress.
5. The U.S. _____ has three branches, or parts.

3. Read and Write Learn to use conjunctions.

and	state **and** national government
or	executive **or** judicial branch
but	Congress **but** not the President

Complete the following sentences. Write them.

1. I want to see the White House, ____*but*____ I don't have time.
2. The President _____ the Vice President are part of the executive branch.
3. Is the Supreme Court in the judicial branch _____ the legislative branch?
4. The three branches are judicial, legislative, _____ executive.
5. Is Congress in the legislative _____ judicial branch?

Now write four sentences. Use conjunctions in them.

Example: I want to visit the White House and the Capitol.

Our World

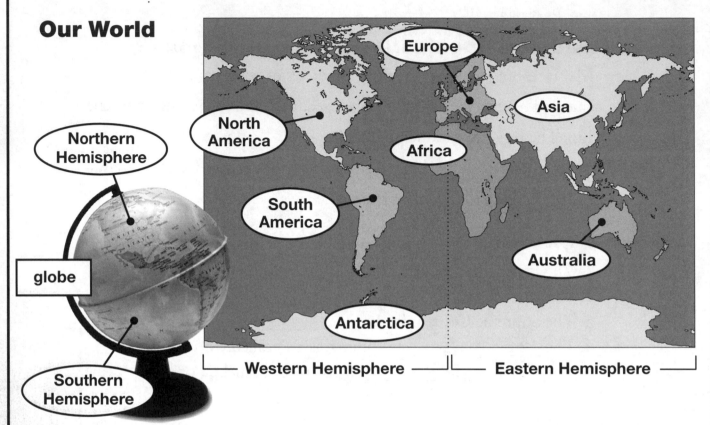

Northern Hemisphere

globe

Southern Hemisphere

Europe

North America

Asia

Africa

South America

Australia

Antarctica

⎣————— Western Hemisphere —————⎦⎣————— Eastern Hemisphere —————⎦

CONCEPTS AND VOCABULARY

 1. Learn New Words Read about world geography.

A **continent** is a large **area** of **land**. The seven continents are the seven largest areas of land on Earth. Their names are Africa, Antarctica, Asia, Australia, Europe, North America, and South America. The continents are found on both halves, or **hemispheres**, of the **globe**.

What continents do you know about? What continent are you living on now? What continents would you like to visit?

Vocabulary

areas
continents
globe
hemispheres
land
Western

Western Hemisphere	Eastern Hemispere
North America	Africa
South America	Asia
part of Antarctica	Australia
	Europe
	part of Antarctica

2. Read and Speak Take turns reading with a partner.

Ms. Jackson: Has anyone ever been to Australia?

Luis: I haven't. Has anyone ever been to Africa?

Susana: I used to live in South America. Now I live in North America.

Lin: I lived in Asia. Asia is a large continent. Europe is a smaller continent.

Lucas: Antarctica is a continent too. It is very far south on the globe.

Complete the following sentences. Use vocabulary words.

1. There are seven _____continents_____ on Earth.
2. A continent is a large area of _____.
3. The continents are the largest _____ of land on Earth.
4. The continents are found in both _____ of the Earth.
5. We live in the _____ Hemisphere.

LANGUAGE DEVELOPMENT

3. Read and Write Learn to combine sentences.

Asia is large. Asia has many people.	Asia is large and has many people.
Europe is small. Europe is a continent.	Europe is a small continent.

On a separate piece of paper, combine these sentences.

1. Asia is big. Africa is big.   *Asia and Africa are big.*
2. Europe is in the north. Asia is in the north.
3. South America is a continent. Australia is a continent.
4. There are seven continents. There are many countries.
5. She lived in South America. She lived in Asia.

Now write four sentences. Combine two sentences to make one.
Example: I want to visit Mexico.
         I want to visit Guatemala.
         I want to visit Mexico and Guatemala.

Vocabulary

Fill in the circle next to the correct definition of the underlined word.

1. César Chávez is an important part of American <u>history</u>.
   - **A** president
   - **B** large town
   - **C** branch of government
   - **D** the story of the past

2. My sister drives a <u>car</u> to get to work.
   - **A** truck
   - **B** something you use to ride on the street
   - **C** bike
   - **D** pay money for

3. Everyone in the U.S. must obey its <u>laws</u>.
   - **A** government
   - **B** legislative branch
   - **C** rules
   - **D** judicial branch

4. Which <u>region</u> of the United States do you live in?
   - **A** globe
   - **B** large area
   - **C** hemisphere
   - **D** one of the seasons

5. A continent is a large piece of <u>land</u>.
   - **A** area that is not water
   - **B** South America
   - **C** North America
   - **D** part of a year

6. In <u>fall</u>, we go back to school.
   - **A** summer
   - **B** month
   - **C** calendar
   - **D** season after summer

Read and Speak

Complete the blanks with _government, continents,_ and _history._
Then read the paragraph out loud.

      In school, we are learning about many things. We learned the names of the seven _____ in English. We are studying important events in the _____ of the United States. We also learned about the three branches of _____. I like learning things in school!

Practice Grammar

Circle the word that best completes the sentence.

    1. He was late to class because he walked too _____.

        slowly   quietly

    2. The executive _____ judicial branches are two of the branches of government.

        and   but

    3. Her teacher's name is _____.

        ms. Ramos   Ms. Ramos

    4. I met my cousin _____ the airport.

        through   at

    5. Can _____ name the four seasons?

        anyone   nothing

Writing

On a separate sheet of paper, combine these sentences.
  The world is big. It has lots of land.

Then write four more sentences about the world. Use _land, area, hemisphere,_ and _continents._

Aa

A.M. *abbreviation* Time between midnight and noon; morning (p. 12).

address *noun* The number, street, town, etc., where you live (p. 32).

alphabet *noun* ABCs; the letters in order (p. 2).

areas *noun* Places (p. 54).

Bb

bike *noun* Something you ride, with two wheels and pedals; bicycle (p. 46).

board *noun* Object on the wall in a classroom, used to write on (p. 8).

body *noun* Your physical form: head, torso, arms, legs, etc. (p. 18).

brother *noun* Boy who has the same parent as you (p. 20).

buildings *noun* Structures; places such as homes, offices, etc. (p. 34).

bus *noun* Something you ride, with other people and a driver (p. 46).

buy *verb* Pay money for; purchase (p. 36).

Cc

calendar *noun* Chart that tells the month, date, year, etc. (p. 26).

car *noun* Something you ride in or drive on a street, with four wheels and an engine (p. 46).

cents *noun* Pennies; parts of a dollar (100 cents = 1 dollar) (p. 38).

city *noun* Large town, place where many people live and work (p. 34).

civil rights *noun* Protections and permissions given by law (p. 50).

clock *noun* Something that tells the time (p. 12).

clothes *noun* Things you wear, such as pants, shirts, shoes (p. 16).

coach *noun* Person who teaches or helps others with a sport (p. 6).

coat *noun* Something you wear over your clothes, in cold weather (p. 16).

computer *noun* An electronic machine that can store and retrieve information (p. 8).

continent *noun* One of seven large masses or areas of land (p. 54).

cost *noun* How much money you pay for something (p. 38).

Dd

day *noun* 24 hours; not night (p. 26).

desk *noun* Furniture you use at school or work, to write at (p. 8).

directions *noun* The way to get to a place; instructions (p. 32).

dollar *noun* American unit of money (p. 38).

drink *verb* To swallow liquid (p. 24).

Ee

earn *verb* To receive money for work done (p. 40).

Earth *noun* The planet on which we live. (p. 30).

eat *verb* To take in food (p. 24).

emotions *noun* Feelings, such as happy and sad (p. 22).

executive *adjective* Branch of federal government, includes the President (p. 52).

experiment *noun* A science test (p. 30).

Ff

fall *noun* One of the four seasons, or part of a year: September, October, November (p. 44).

family *noun* Related people; people who live together as a group (p. 20).

father *noun* Male head of a family; male parent (p. 20).

feel *verb* Have or experience happiness, sadness, etc. (p. 22).

food *noun* What you eat (p. 24).

friend *noun* Person you know well and like a lot (p. 4).

Gg

globe *noun* Earth, or a round model of Earth (p. 54).

government *noun* The authorities or heads of something, like a country (p. 52).

Hh

happy *adjective* A feeling: not sad (p. 22).

hear *verb* To sense sounds with your ears; listen; one of the five senses (p. 18).

hello *noun* Greeting; hi (p. 4).

hemisphere *noun* Half of Earth (p. 54).

history *noun* Story of the past (p. 50).

hungry *adjective* Feeling that you need or want to eat (p. 24).

Ii

individuals *noun* People (p. 50).

Jj

job *noun* Work; something you do to earn money (p. 40).

judicial *adjective* Branch of federal government, includes the Supreme Court (p. 52).

Kk

keyboard *noun* Set of keys on a computer, typewriter, or piano (p. 8).

Ll

land *noun* Area of Earth that is not water (p. 54).

laws *noun* The rules we live by (p. 52).

legislative *adjective* Branch of federal government, includes Congress (p. 52).

librarian *noun* Person who works in a library (p. 6).

line up *verb* Stand up and get in order (p. 10).

live *verb* Exist; stay at (p. 32).

Mm

map *noun* Drawing of streets or area; drawing that shows how to get somewhere (pp. 30, 32).

measure *verb* To find the size of something (p. 30).

meet *verb* Come together for the first time (p. 4).

midnight *noun* 12:00 A.M.; 12:00 at night (p. 12).

Midwest *noun* U.S. region that includes Illinois, Indiana, Iowa, Kansas, Michigan, Minnesota, Missouri, Nebraska, North Dakota, Ohio, South Dakota, Wisconsin (p. 48).

money *noun* What you use to pay for things; dollars and cents (p. 38).

month *noun* One of twelve divisions of the year, for example, January (p. 26).

mother *noun* Female head of a family; female parent (p. 20).

Nn

name *noun* What you are called; what anything is called (p. 4).

need *verb* Must have; have to have (p. 36).

noon *noun* 12:00 P.M.; 12:00 in the day (p. 12).

Northeast *noun* U.S. region that includes Connecticut, Delaware, Maine, Maryland, Massachusetts, New Hampshire, New Jersey, New York, Pennsylvania, Rhode Island, Vermont (p. 48).

numbers *noun* 1, 2, 3, etc. (p. 2).

nurse *noun* Person who helps doctors take care of people (p. 6).

Oo

office *noun* A room where people work, usually sitting at desks (p. 6).

Pp

P.M. *abbreviation* Time between noon and midnight; afternoon (p. 12).

pants *noun* Clothes you wear on the bottom part of your body (p. 16).

people *noun* Human beings (p. 34).

plane *noun* Something you travel on, through the air (p. 46).

police officer *noun* Person whose job is to protect and keep order (p. 40).

presidents *noun* The people who are or have been the head of state. (p. 50).

price *noun* How much money you have to pay for something (p. 38).

principal *noun* The head of a school (p. 6).

put away *verb* Remove; stop using (p. 10).

Qq

quarter *noun* A coin equal to 25 cents. One of four equal parts (p. 38).

Rr

raise *verb* Put up (p.10).

region *noun* Large area in one place; group of states (p. 48).

Ss

sad *adjective* Not happy (p. 22).

seasons *noun* Four parts of a year: fall, winter, spring, summer (p. 44).

see *verb* Take in with your eyes; one of the five senses (p. 18).

sell *verb* Trade something for money (p. 40).

shirt *noun* Clothes you wear on the top part of your body (p. 16).

shoes *noun* Things you wear on your feet, over socks (p. 16).

shopping *verb* Buying things at a store (p. 36).

sister *noun* Girl who has the same parent as you (p. 20).

smell *verb* Take in through the nose; one of the five senses (p. 18).

smile *verb* Look happy (p. 22).

solve *verb* To find the correct answer to a problem (p. 30).

Southeast *noun* U.S. region that includes Alabama, Arkansas, Florida, Georgia, Kentucky, Louisiana, Mississippi, North Carolina, South Carolina, Tennessee, Virginia, West

Virginia, and Washington, D.C. (p. 48).

Southwest *noun* U.S. region that includes Arizona, New Mexico, Oklahoma, Texas (p. 48).

spend *verb* Use money to buy things (p. 36).

spring *noun* One of the four seasons, or parts of the year: March, April, May (p. 44).

store *noun* A place where you can buy things (p. 36).

street *noun* Route, way (p. 32).

student *noun* Person who studies (p. 6).

suburb *noun* Residential area outside a big city (p. 34).

summer *noun* One of the four seasons, or part of a year: June, July, August (p. 44).

symbols *noun* Things that mean, or stand for, something else (p. 50).

Tt

take out *verb* Put on the outside; get ready for use (p. 10).

taste *verb* Take in through the mouth; one of the five senses (p. 18).

teacher *noun* Someone who gives lessons (p. 6).

textbook *noun* Special book for school (p. 8).

thank you *noun* A way to say you are glad for help (p. 4).

thirsty *adjective* Feeling that you need or want to drink (p. 24).

time *noun* How we measure the length of days, hours, minutes, etc. (p. 12).

touch *verb* Take in through the fingers, skin, feeling; one of the five senses (p. 18).

town *noun* Place where people live and work together; smaller than a city (p. 34).

transportation *noun* Ways to travel, such as by bike, car, bus, plane (p. 46).

Uu

United States of America *noun* The country where we live (p. 48).

Vv

vegetable *noun* Plant grown to be used as food (p. 24).

Ww

wait *verb* Stay; don't go (p. 10).

week *noun* Seven days: Monday, Tuesday, Wednesday, Thursday, Friday, Saturday, Sunday (p. 26).

West *noun* U.S. region that includes Alaska, California, Colorado, Hawaii, Idaho, Montana, Nevada, Oregon, Utah, Washington, Wyoming (p. 48).

winter *noun* One of the four seasons, or part of a year: December, January, February (p. 44).

worker *noun* Someone who does a job (p. 40).

Xx

x-ray *noun* A photograph of the inside of a person's body (p.40).

Yy

year *noun* 12 months (p. 26).

Zz

zero *noun* The number 0. Nothing (p. 2).